Sanjeev Kapoor

The Best of Wraps 'N' Rolls

In association with Alyona Kapoor

Popular Prakashan

www.popularprakashan.com

Published by
POPULAR PRAKASHAN PVT. LTD.
301, Mahalaxmi Chambers
22, Bhulabhai Desai Road
Mumbai - 400 026

First Published 2017

(4479)
ISBN: 978-81-7991-920-0

Design: Anjali Sawant
Typesetting: Satyawan Rane

PRINTED IN INDIA
by Saurabh Printers (P) Ltd.
Plot No. 67 A-68, Ecotech, Ext. I
Kasna, Greater Noida-201306 (U.P)

Author's Note

A lot of creative thinking has gone into making this collection of wrap and roll recipes. In *The Best of Wraps 'N' Rolls,* I have compiled numerous options for healthy snacks which take away the 'junk' from junk food. These recipes are wholesome and are mini-meals in themselves.

For vegetarians, there are Baked Corn Rolls, Manchurian Rolls and more. Non-vegetarians can choose from Chicken Calzones, Hot Dogs and many others. For people with a sweet tooth there are Swiss Rolls, Cinnamon Rolls to name a few.

All the recipes serve four portions. Go ahead and enjoy these delicious recipes with your loved ones!

Happy cooking!

Contents

VEGETARIAN

NON-VEGETARIAN

DESSERTS

Manchurian Rolls

Ingredients

4 crusty bread rolls

1 medium cabbage, grated

1 medium carrot, grated

¼ small cauliflower, grated

3 medium spring onions with greens, chopped

¼ cup refined flour

¼ cup cornflour

Salt to taste

Oil for deep-frying

Sauce

2 tablespoons oil

1 inch fresh ginger, chopped

4-6 garlic cloves, chopped

2 inches celery stalk, chopped

3 green chillies, chopped

2 tablespoons light soy sauce

1 teaspoon sugar

¼ teaspoon MSG (optional)

1 cup Vegetable Stock (page 96)

2 tablespoons cornflour

1 tablespoon white vinegar

Salt to taste

Method

- Mix the cabbage, carrot and cauliflower in a bowl and thoroughly rub in one teaspoon of salt. Add the spring onions, refined flour and cornflour. Mix thoroughly. Shape into lemon-sized balls.
- Heat sufficient oil in a wok and deep-fry the vegetable balls in small batches over a medium heat for three to four minutes or until golden brown. Drain on absorbent paper.
- For the sauce, heat two tablespoons of oil in a wok or a non-stick pan and stir-fry the ginger and garlic for one minute. Add the celery and green chillies and stir-fry for one minute longer.
- Add the soy sauce, sugar, MSG and salt to taste. Stir in the vegetable stock and bring to a boil.
- Mix two tablespoons of cornflour with half a cup of water and stir into the hot stock. Cook, stirring continuously, for a couple of minutes or until the sauce starts to thicken.
- Add the fried vegetable balls and vinegar and mix well.
- Slit open the rolls and fill with the vegetable balls and sauce. Serve immediately.

Bread Rolls

Ingredients

8 large slices of bread, crusts removed
1½ cups grated mozzarella cheese
1 medium onion, finely chopped
3 tablespoons chopped fresh coriander
1 green chilli, finely chopped
Salt to taste
Oil for deep-frying

To serve

Mint Chutney (page 60)

Method

- In a bowl, combine the mozzarella cheese, onion, fresh coriander, green chilli and salt.
- Soak the slices of bread, one at a time, in water for about ten seconds. Squeeze out the excess water by gently pressing between your palms.
- Place each slice on the worktop, place some of the cheese mixture at one end and roll the bread up firmly to cover the stuffing completely, ensuring that the edges are well sealed.
- Heat sufficient oil in a deep pan and deep-fry the rolls until golden brown. Drain on absorbent paper. Serve hot with tomato ketchup or mint chutney.

Sago-Potato Rolls

Ingredients

¾ cup sago
3 large potatoes, boiled, peeled and mashed
½ cup roasted and peeled peanuts, crushed
3 green chillies, chopped
1 inch ginger, chopped
1 tablespoon lemon juice
2-3 tablespoons chopped fresh coriander
Salt to taste
Oil for deep-frying

To serve

Green Chutney (page 95)

Method

- Wash the sago and soak in water for at least one hour. If in a hurry, soak the sago in hot water till they swell. Squeeze out and place in a large bowl.
- Add the potatoes, peanuts, green chillies, ginger, lemon juice, fresh coriander and salt and mix well. Add a little water if necessary and make a dough. Let it stand for a few minutes.

- Divide the dough into eight equal portions and shape into oval rolls.
- Heat sufficient oil in a non-stick kadai till medium hot. Slide in four rolls at a time and deep-fry till golden brown. Drain on absorbent paper.
- Serve hot with green chutney.

Note: *For a non-vegetarian version, you can substitute cooked minced meat (keema) for the mashed potatoes.*

Baked Corn Rolls

Ingredients

12 slices of bread with the crusts removed

1 cup boiled sweetcorn

1 large potato, boiled and mashed

2 green chillies, chopped

1 teaspoon ginger paste

¼ cup chopped fresh coriander

1 teaspoon lemon juice

Salt to taste

2 tablespoons oil

1 large onion, chopped

To serve

Green Chutney (page 95)

Method

- Preheat the oven to 180°C/350°F/Gas Mark 4.
- Coarsely crush the boiled sweetcorn in a blender. Transfer into a bowl.
- Add the potato, green chillies, ginger paste, fresh coriander, lemon juice and salt and mix well.
- Heat the oil in a non-stick pan and sauté the onion till light brown. Add to the corn mixture and mix well. Divide the mixture into twelve equal portions and shape each one into an oval and set aside.
- Soak the slices of bread, one at a time, in water for about ten seconds. Squeeze out the excess water by gently pressing each slice between your palms. Place a potato-corn oval at one end of each slice and roll firmly to enclose the oval completely.
- Place the rolls on a greased baking tray. Bake for approximately twelve minutes or till the rolls turn light brown.
- Serve hot with tomato ketchup or green chutney.

Cabbage Rolls

Ingredients

8 cabbage leaves

4 medium potatoes, boiled, peeled and mashed

½ cup green peas, boiled and mashed

1 teaspoon chaat masala

1 cup gram flour

½ teaspoon red chilli powder

½ teaspoon soda bicarbonate

Salt to taste

Oil for deep-frying

To serve

Mint Chutney (page 60)

Method

- Blanch the cabbage leaves in boiling salted water. Drain and pat dry with absorbent paper.
- Mix the potatoes, green peas, salt and chaat masala in a bowl. Divide the mixture into eight equal portions.

- Place each portion of the mixture at one end of each cabbage leaf. Fold the sides around the filling and roll up the leaves firmly.
- Make a batter of coating consistency with the gram flour, chilli powder, salt, soda bicarbonate and some water.
- Heat sufficient oil in a non-stick kadai. Dip the cabbage rolls in the batter and deep-fry until golden brown. Drain on absorbent paper.
- Serve hot with tomato ketchup or mint chutney.

Cheesy Spinach Rolls

Ingredients

¼ cup grated processed cheese

2 medium bunches (700 grams) spinach, blanched and chopped

1½ cups whole-wheat flour

2 garlic cloves, chopped

2 green chillies, finely chopped

½ teaspoon garam masala powder

Salt to taste

3 tablespoons oil + for shallow-frying

Method

- Mix the flour with salt and two tablespoons of oil.
- Add sufficient water and knead to make a soft dough. Divide into four portions and roll out each portion into a thin chapati. Heat a non-stick tawa, roast the chapati lightly and set aside.
- For the filling, heat one tablespoon of oil in a non-stick pan. Add the garlic and sauté for a minute. Add the spinach, green chillies, salt and garam masala powder, and mix well.
- Heat each chapati on the tawa. Spread half the spinach mixture over it and top with half the cheese. Place another chapati on top.
- Drizzle a little oil all around and cook for a few minutes. Flip over and drizzle a little more oil all around. Cook till both sides are evenly golden brown and crisp.
- Cut into wedges and serve hot.

Vegetable Frankies

Ingredients

4 refined flour roti

1 medium carrot, grated

¼ cup shelled green peas, parboiled and crushed

2 large potatoes, boiled, peeled and mashed

½ teaspoon cumin seeds

½ inch ginger, finely chopped

1 green chilli, finely chopped

¼ teaspoon red chilli powder

A pinch of turmeric powder

¼ teaspoon garam masala powder

1 tablespoon chopped fresh coriander

½ teaspoon dried mango powder

Salt to taste

1 tablespoon oil + for shallow-frying

To serve

4 teaspoons Green Chutney (page 95)

1 medium onion, sliced

1 teaspoon vinegar

Chaat masala, as required

Method

- Heat one tablespoon oil in a non-stick pan; add the cumin seeds and sauté lightly.
- Add the carrot, green peas, ginger, green chilli, chilli powder, turmeric powder, garam masala powder and salt, and sauté over medium heat for two minutes. Transfer to a plate and cool.
- Add the mashed potatoes, fresh coriander and dried mango powder to the cooled mixture and mix well. Adjust seasoning.
- Divide the mixture into eight portions and shape into four-inch long cylinders. Shallow-fry the rolls in sufficient hot oil till golden brown. Drain on absorbent paper and set aside.
- To prepare the frankies, place each roti on a flat working surface and spread a teaspoon of green chutney all over the roti. Place a potato roll on one side.
- Sprinkle some of the sliced onions, drizzle one-fourth teaspoon of vinegar, sprinkle chaat masala over and roll up firmly.
- Wrap in aluminium foil and serve immediately.

Middle-Eastern Wraps

Ingredients

4 whole-wheat roti

1½ teaspoons tahini

½ cup yogurt

5-6 fresh mint leaves, roughly torn

1 medium onion, quartered

½ medium zucchini, sliced

1 medium carrot, sliced

1 medium green capsicum, cut into thick strips

2 teaspoons lemon juice

1 teaspoon mixed dried herbs

1 teaspoons red chilli flakes

A few sprigs of fresh parsley, chopped

Salt to taste

3 tablespoons olive oil

Method

- Mix the tahini, yogurt, salt and fresh mint in a small bowl and set aside.
- Marinate the onion, zucchini, carrot and capsicum in a mixture of olive oil, lemon juice, mixed herbs, chilli flakes and salt for about fifteen minutes.

- Grill the vegetables on a hot grill till the grill marks are seen on the pieces. Remove and divide into four portions.
- To assemble the rolls, spread the tahini mixture on each roti, top with a portion of vegetables, sprinkle with parsley and roll up tightly.
- Serve immediately.

Tortilla Rolls

Ingredients

4 ten-inch whole-wheat tortillas

3 tablespoons cream cheese

¼ cup yogurt

1 teaspoon red chilli sauce

1 small red capsicum, finely chopped

1 small green capsicum, finely chopped

¼ cup sweetcorn kernels, boiled

1 medium onion, chopped

1 teaspoon lemon juice

1 tablespoon chopped fresh coriander

2-3 garlic cloves, finely chopped

Salt to taste

Method

- In a bowl, mix together the cream cheese, yogurt, red chilli sauce, red capsicum, green capsicum, sweetcorn, onion, salt, lemon juice, fresh coriander and garlic. Divide the mixture into four equal portions.
- Place each tortilla on the worktop, spread one portion of the mixture evenly over it and roll up tightly. Wrap in foil and place in a refrigerator to chill for half an hour.
- When ready to serve, remove the foil and slice each roll diagonally into two-inch thick slices and serve chilled.

Note: You can use cooked chicken or chicken tikka cut into small pieces for a non-vegetarian version.

Vegetable Spring Rolls

Ingredients

Spring roll wrappers

1 cup + 3 tablespoons cornflour

¼ cup refined flour

Salt to taste

Oil for deep-frying

Filling

1 medium onion, thinly sliced

2 medium carrots, grated

1 medium green capsicum, cut into thin strips

½ small cabbage, finely shredded

1 tablespoon light soy sauce

¼ teaspoon white pepper powder

¾ cup bean sprouts

2 spring onions with greens, finely sliced

Salt to taste

2 tablespoons oil

Method

- To make the filling, heat two tablespoons of oil in a wok, add the onion and carrots and stir-fry for half a minute.

- Add the capsicum and cabbage and continue to stir-fry for one minute. Add the soy sauce, white pepper powder and salt. Add the bean sprouts and spring onions with the greens and stir-fry for about half a minute. Remove from heat and cool the filling to room temperature.
- To make the spring roll wrappers, mix one cup of cornflour, refined flour and salt to taste in a mixing bowl. Add two cups of water and whisk thoroughly. Strain the batter and set aside for fifteen minutes. Adjust the consistency of the batter by adding a little water if required.
- Heat an eight-inch non-stick frying pan, brush with a little oil and pour a ladleful of batter into it. Swirl to coat the bottom of the pan and pour the excess batter back into the bowl. Cook over medium heat till the edges start curling. Peel off or remove in one swift motion. Cool and sprinkle with a little cornflour. Repeat the process to make eight to ten wrappers.
- Mix one tablespoon of cornflour and two tablespoons of water to make a paste. Divide filling into eight to ten equal portions. Place a portion of filling at one end of each wrapper and roll up tightly, folding the sides in while you roll. Seal the ends with the cornflour paste.
- Heat sufficient oil in a wok; deep-fry two spring rolls at a time turning frequently, till crisp and golden brown. Drain on absorbent paper.
- Cut each spring roll into four pieces and serve hot with Sichuan Sauce (page 96).

Satay Wraps

Ingredients

2 cups tofu cubes

1 red capsicum, sliced

1 zucchini, sliced

7-8 fresh button mushrooms, sliced

5-6 slices of tinned pineapple, quartered

2 garlic cloves, sliced

½ cup bean sprouts

1 tablespoon olive oil

Pancake batter

1 cup refined flour

¼ cup milk

A pinch of salt

4 teaspoons oil + for greasing

Satay sauce

¼ cup roasted peanuts, coarsely powdered

4 garlic cloves, chopped
1 small onion, grated
½ teaspoon red chilli powder
1 tablespoon dark soy sauce
3 tablespoons tomato purée
2 teaspoons honey
Salt to taste
1 teaspoon oil

Method

- Preheat the oven to 180°C/350°F/Gas Mark 4.
- To make the satay sauce, heat the oil in a non-stick pan and add the garlic and onion. Sauté over high heat, for half a minute.
- Add the chilli powder and then immediately add the dark soy sauce, tomato purée, honey, crushed peanuts, salt and one cup of water.
- Bring the mixture to a boil and simmer for five minutes, stirring occasionally. Remove from heat and set aside.
- To make the pancake batter, blend together the flour, a pinch of salt, milk and water as required and whisk well so that no lumps form. Add four teaspoons of oil and whisk till smooth.

- Lightly grease a non-stick frying pan and heat till moderately hot. Pour a ladleful of batter and rotate the pan to spread it evenly. Cook till done. Similarly make the remaining pancakes.
- Generously apply the satay sauce with a pastry brush to the tofu, capsicum, zucchini, mushrooms and pineapple pieces.
- Roast in the oven for about twenty minutes, turning occasionally. Meanwhile sauté the garlic in olive oil until fragrant.
- Place the roasted vegetables and tofu on the pancakes. Top with bean sprouts and fried garlic. Roll up the pancakes tightly.
- Slice each pancake into several pieces and serve with the remaining satay sauce.

Teriyaki Rolls

Ingredients

4 medium crusty bread rolls
2 medium green capsicums, sliced
10 fresh button mushrooms, sliced
1 large onion, sliced
½ cup tofu cubes
1 tablespoon olive oil

Teriyaki sauce

2 tablespoons butter
1 inch ginger, sliced
1 medium onion, finely chopped
½ cup white wine
12-15 black grapes, roughly crushed by hand
1 tablespoon soy sauce
½ teaspoon black pepper powder
1 tablespoon molasses
2 tablespoons honey
Salt to taste

Method

- To make the teriyaki sauce, heat the butter in a non-stick pan. Add the ginger and onion and sauté till golden brown.
- Add the white wine and cook till the mixture reduces a little.
- Add the crushed black grapes and continue to cook, stirring, for five to seven minutes till the grapes are soft.
- Add the soy sauce, pepper powder, salt, molasses and honey. Mix well and strain.
- Heat the olive oil in a non-stick pan; add the capsicums, mushrooms, onion and tofu and toss for two minutes.
- Stir in the teriyaki sauce and cook for two minutes. Divide the mixture into four portions.
- Cut the crusty rolls in half and spread one portion of the vegetable and tofu mixture on one half of each roll and cover with the other half.
- Serve immediately.

Potato Rolls

Ingredients

4 large potatoes, boiled, peeled and mashed

4 bread slices

½ teaspoon black pepper powder

10 cashew nuts, coarsely pounded

2 green chillies, finely chopped

1 inch ginger, finely chopped

½ cup shelled green peas, blanched and coarsely ground

2 tablespoons chopped fresh coriander

Tomato ketchup, as required

Salt to taste

¼ cup ghee + for shallow-frying

Method

- Crumble the bread to make fine breadcrumbs. Mix with the potatoes, salt and pepper powder to make a dough. Divide into eight equal portions.
- Grease your palm with ghee and roll the dough into balls.
- Mix together the cashew nuts, green chillies, ginger, green peas, fresh coriander and salt. Divide into eight equal portions.

- Take each potato ball in your palm and make a hollow in it. Place a portion of the cashew nut stuffing in the centre and gather the edges together to cover the stuffing. Shape into an oblong roll.
- Heat sufficient ghee in a flat non-stick frying pan. Lower heat and place four rolls at a time on it. Shallow-fry till the rolls are evenly golden brown on all sides. Drain on absorbent paper.
- Serve hot with tomato ketchup.

Corn and Bean Burritos

Ingredients

100 grams sweetcorn kernels
250 grams sprouted beans, blanched
4 refined flour tortillas
½ cup grated mozzarella cheese
10-12 black peppercorns, crushed
1 tablespoon lemon juice
1 medium tomato, chopped
½ cup shredded lettuce

2 spring onions, chopped
2 green chillies, chopped
½ cup Salsa (page 51)
Salt to taste
Chilled sour cream, to serve

Method

- Preheat the oven to 200°C/400°F/Gas Mark 6.
- Mix the cheese, salt, crushed peppercorns, lemon juice and sprouted beans in a bowl.
- In another bowl, mix together the tomato, lettuce and spring onions thoroughly. Add the corn and green chillies and mix.
- Place the tortillas on a plate. Layer equal portions of the cheese and bean mixture and the corn and tomato mixture on each tortilla. Sprinkle the salsa on top and fold each tortilla over.
- Arrange the tortillas in a baking dish and bake for twenty minutes.
- Serve hot with the chilled sour cream.

Spicy Moroccan Wraps

Ingredients

4 cornmeal (page 49) or whole-wheat tortillas

1 large green zucchini, cut into ½-inch cubes

2 medium yellow capsicums, cut into ½-inch squares

¼ teaspoon red chilli flakes

¼ teaspoon black pepper powder

¼ teaspoon mixed dried herbs

10-12 green or black olives, chopped

½ cup sun-dried tomatoes, soaked in water and chopped

1 tablespoon chopped fresh parsley

Salt to taste

2 tablespoons olive oil

Harrisa sauce

6 dried red chillies

1 teaspoon coriander seeds

1 teaspoon caraway seeds

1 teaspoon cumin seeds

1 garlic clove, minced

1 tablespoon vinegar

Salt to taste

Method

- To make the harrisa sauce, soak the red chillies in one cup of water for ten minutes.
- Dry-roast the coriander seeds, caraway seeds and cumin seeds till fragrant and grind them with the red chillies. Transfer the mixture to a bowl, add the garlic, vinegar and salt and mix well.
- Preheat the oven to 180°C/350°F/Gas Mark 4.
- Marinate the zucchini and yellow capsicums in a mixture of olive oil, chilli flakes, salt, pepper powder and mixed herbs for ten minutes.
- Roast the vegetables in the oven for twenty minutes.
- Add the olives, sun-dried tomatoes and parsley to the roasted vegetables and mix. Stir in the harrisa sauce.
- Spread the mixture equally over the tortillas and roll up firmly.
- Serve immediately.

Garden Wraps

Ingredients

4 refined flour tortillas

½ cup cream cheese

1 cup shredded iceberg lettuce

1 medium onion, sliced

2 medium cucumbers, cut into thin strips

2 medium tomatoes, cut into thin strips

½ cup bean sprouts

1 teaspoon red chilli flakes

Salt to taste

Method

- Spread the cream cheese on the tortillas.
- Top with the lettuce, onion, cucumbers, tomatoes and bean sprouts. Sprinkle the chilli flakes and salt on top.
- Roll up each tortilla tightly. Cut in half and serve immediately.

Vegetable Papad Rolls

Ingredients

8 medium urad papads

1 medium carrot, chopped

1 medium potato, chopped

6 French beans, chopped

100 grams cauliflower, chopped

1 medium tomato, chopped

½ teaspoon turmeric powder

½ teaspoon red chilli powder

1 tablespoon chopped fresh coriander

Salt to taste

1 tablespoon oil + for deep-frying

Method

- Boil the carrot, potato, French beans and cauliflower with a pinch of salt till three-fourth cooked. Drain water and spread the vegetables out to dry.
- Heat one tablespoon of oil in a non-stick pan and sauté the tomato. Add the boiled vegetables and sauté for a while. Add the turmeric powder and chilli powder and mix well. Add the fresh coriander, remove from heat and set aside to cool.

- Dip each papad in water so that it becomes pliable. Spoon a little mixture along the centre and roll the papad up like a dosa. Press the ends well to seal.
- Heat sufficient oil in a non-stick kadai till it starts smoking. Deep-fry the papad rolls on both sides till crisp. Drain on absorbent paper.
- Serve hot.

Spiral Snack Rolls

Ingredients

3 cups refined flour + for dusting

1½ teaspoons dried yeast

2 teaspoons sugar

30 grams butter

1½ teaspoons salt

Filling

3 medium potatoes, boiled, peeled and chopped

2 medium onions, chopped

2 medium tomatoes, chopped

½ cup green peas

½ teaspoon cumin seeds
1 teaspoon ginger paste
1 teaspoon garlic paste
2 green chillies, chopped
½ teaspoon red chilli powder
1 teaspoon pav bhaji masala
Salt to taste
2 tablespoons oil

Method

- Sift flour and salt together into a bowl.
- Mix yeast and sugar in a small bowl. Add one-fourth cup of lukewarm water and set aside till it begins to froth.
- Add the yeast mixture to the flour and knead, adding water, a little at a time, till you use up one cup of water. Keep stretching the dough from time to time and kneading it till you get a smooth and elastic dough. Cover with a damp cloth and set it aside in a warm place till it doubles in size.
- For the filling, heat oil in a non-stick pan, add cumin seeds. When they begin to change colour add ginger paste, garlic paste, green chillies and onions and sauté till the onions are translucent.
- Add the tomatoes and green peas and sauté till peas are cooked. Add the chilli powder, pav bhaji masala, salt and potatoes and mix. Remove from heat and let it cool.

- Lightly dust the rolling pin with flour and roll the dough into a rectangle about thirty by sixty centimetres. Spread the filling evenly.
- Starting at the narrow end, roll the dough as tightly as you can towards the other end. Pinch the seam to seal it. Cut the roll diagonally into eight equal pieces.
- Grease a large baking tray. Arrange the pieces, cut side down, on the tray. Cover tightly with a cling film. Place in a warm place for about one-and-a-half hours or till the pieces double in size.
- Preheat oven 190°C/375°F/Gas Mark 5.
- Remove the cling film and place the baking tray in the preheated oven and bake for twenty-five to thirty minutes. The rolls should be golden brown yet very soft to touch.
- Once done, remove and brush with melted butter and leave them on a wire rack to cool. Slice diagonally and serve.

Oriental Wraps

Ingredients

2 pita breads

1 cup tofu cubes

Chilli-garlic sauce, as required

½ cup shredded red cabbage

½ cup shredded carrot

2 spring onions with greens, sliced

Sesame dressing

2 tablespoon roasted sesame seeds

¼ inch ginger

1 garlic clove

1 tablespoon soy sauce

2 tablespoons rice wine vinegar

2 teaspoons sugar

Salt to taste

Method

- For the dressing, powder the sesame seeds in a blender. Add the ginger and garlic and blend for half a minute. Add the soy sauce, rice wine vinegar, salt and sugar and blend some more. If the mixture is too thick, add a little water. Transfer the dressing to a bowl.
- Preheat the oven to 200°C/400°F/Gas Mark 6.

- Marinate the tofu cubes in two tablespoons of sesame dressing for fifteen minutes.
- Place the tofu on a baking sheet and bake for thirty minutes. Reserve the remaining dressing. Take the tofu out of the oven and set aside to cool.
- Spread the chilli-garlic sauce on each pita bread. Place a layer each of red cabbage and carrots and spring onions with greens on top. Arrange the baked tofu over the vegetables.
- Drizzle the remaining dressing over the tofu. Roll up and cut each pita bread into half.
- Serve immediately.

Ratatouille Wraps

Ingredients

4 pita breads

2 medium onions, chopped

2 garlic cloves, finely chopped

1 red capsicum, cut into ½-inch squares

2 small zucchini, cut into ½-inch cubes

3 small brinjals, chopped

2 tomatoes, chopped

1 tablespoon chopped fresh parsley

Black pepper powder to taste
¼ teaspoon red chilli flakes
¼ teaspoon dried oregano
Salt to taste
2 tablespoons olive oil

Method

- To make the ratatouille, heat the olive oil in a non-stick pan. Add the onions and garlic and sauté for five minutes or until soft. Add the capsicum, zucchini and brinjals and cook for five more minutes. Add the tomatoes and half a cup of water.
- Cover the pan and cook for fifteen minutes. Uncover occasionally and stir gently. Add the parsley during the last three to four minutes of cooking.
- Add the salt, pepper powder, red chilli flakes and oregano and mix well.
- Cut each pita bread in half and open out the pocket.
- Spoon the ratatouille into the pita pockets and serve immediately.

Pizza Margherita Wraps

Ingredients

4 pita breads

1 cup pizza sauce

16 tomato slices

4 thick slices of mozzarella cheese

2 tablespoons shredded fresh basil

1 tablespoon olive oil

Method

- Slice each pita bread vertically into two.
- Spread some pizza sauce on one slice. Arrange the tomato slices over the sauce followed by one slice of cheese.
- Sprinkle fresh basil and cover with the other slice of pita bread. Apply some olive oil on top of each slice. Grill until brown on both sides.
- Serve immediately.

Quesadillas

Ingredients

Tortillas

1 cup cornmeal

½ cup refined flour

¼ cup milk

Salt to taste

Filling

2 medium onions, chopped

6-8 garlic cloves, chopped

2 cups red kidney beans, boiled

6 tablespoons tomato ketchup

4 green chillies, chopped

2 teaspoons paprika

2 cups grated processed cheese

4 tablespoons fresh coriander, chopped

Salt to taste

2 tablespoons olive oil

Method

- Mix together the cornmeal, refined flour and salt. Knead into a soft dough with milk and half a cup of water. Cover with a damp piece of muslin and set aside for a few minutes.
- Divide the dough into eight equal portions and roll out each portion into a thin ten-inch round tortilla (chapati). Lightly cook each tortilla on both sides on a hot non-stick tawa and set aside.
- To make the filling, heat one tablespoon of olive oil in a non-stick pan and sauté the onions and garlic for one minute.
- Add the boiled kidney beans, tomato ketchup, green chillies, paprika and salt and cook for two to three minutes.
- To make the quesadillas, heat a non-stick tawa and place a tortilla on it. Spread one-fourth portion of the filling, and top with one-fourth portion of the cheese and fresh coriander. Cover with another tortilla. Drizzle some olive oil all around.
- Turn the tortilla over gently when the underside has cooked. Cook the other side.
- Remove, cut into wedges and serve hot.

Santa Fé Wraps

Ingredients

2 Corn Tortillas (page 49)
2 cups fresh corn kernels
1 medium zucchini, chopped
½ cup tinned black beans, mashed
¼ cup sour cream
½ cup grated processed cheese
Salt to taste
1 tablespoon olive oil

Salsa

2 large onions, halved
5 garlic cloves, halved
4 medium tomatoes, halved
1 green capsicum, quartered
1 tablespoon lemon juice
Salt to taste

Method

- To make the salsa, place the onions, garlic, tomatoes and capsicum on a hot griddle and roast till the skins are charred.
- Cool and grind coarsely with salt. Transfer to a bowl and stir in the lemon juice. Set aside.

- Preheat the oven to 200°C/400°F/Gas Mark 6.
- Mix together the corn, zucchini, salt and olive oil in a bowl. Transfer the mixture to an ovenproof pan and roast it in the oven for fifteen minutes.
- Spread the mashed black beans over each tortilla. Spread a layer of sour cream on top. Arrange the roasted corn and zucchini over the sour cream.
- Spread the salsa and cheese on top of the corn-zucchini layer. Roll up the tortillas, cut each in half and serve immediately.

Mutton Frankies

Ingredients

350 grams boneless mutton, cut into ½-inch thin pieces

1½ cups refined flour

3 large onions

2 teaspoons ginger paste

2 teaspoons garlic paste

2 teaspoons coriander powder

½ teaspoon turmeric powder

2 teaspoons red chilli powder

2 large tomatoes, chopped

2 tablespoons fresh coriander, finely chopped

½ teaspoon garam masala powder

3 eggs, beaten

4 teaspoons chilli vinegar

Salt to taste

2 tablespoons oil

Method

- Roughly chop two onions and slice the remaining one.
- Mix the refined flour and salt in a bowl. Add sufficient water and knead into a soft dough.

- Heat two tablespoons of oil in a pressure cooker. Add the roughly chopped onion and sauté for two minutes. Add the ginger paste, garlic paste and continue to sauté for another minute.
- Add the mutton pieces and sauté for two to three minutes. Add the salt, coriander powder, turmeric powder and chilli powder and mix.
- Add the tomatoes and sauté for two to three minutes. Add a quarter cup of water. When the mixture comes to a boil, close the lid of the pressure cooker and cook under pressure till the pressure is released five or six times (five or six whistles).
- Remove the lid when the pressure has reduced completely. Stir in the fresh coriander and garam masala powder and cook till the mixture is dry.
- Divide the dough into eight equal portions and roll out into roti. Cook each roti, on a hot non-stick tawa till almost done.
- Pour some beaten egg over the roti and cook till set. Turn over to cook the other side.
- Place the roti, egg side up, on a serving plate. Place some of the mutton mixture at one end. Sprinkle some onion over the mutton. Drizzle some chilli vinegar and roll up firmly. Serve immediately.

Masala Keema Rolls

Ingredients

Masala keema

500 grams minced mutton

¾ cup skimmed milk yogurt

1 tablespoon garlic paste

½ tablespoon ginger paste

1 teaspoon red chilli powder

½ teaspoon garam masala powder

8 teaspoons Green Chutney (page 95)

1 teaspoon chilli sauce

1 teaspoon tomato sauce

2 medium onions, sliced into rings

2 tablespoons lemon juice

2 teaspoons chaat masala

Salt to taste

2 tablespoons oil

Roti

1½ cups whole-wheat flour

3 tablespoons skimmed milk yogurt

Salt to taste

Method

- Mix together the yogurt, garlic paste, ginger paste, chilli powder, garam masala powder and salt.
- Marinate the mutton mince in the mixture for thirty to forty minutes.
- Heat the oil in a non-stick pan. Add the marinated mince and cook over medium heat till the mince is cooked and dry. Divide into eight equal portions.
- In another bowl, mix together the whole-wheat flour, yogurt and salt. Add sufficient water and knead into a soft dough. Cover the dough with a damp piece of muslin and allow it to rest for eight to ten minutes.
- Divide the dough into eight equal portions. Roll out each portion into a seven-inch roti.
- Heat a non-stick tawa; place each roti on it and roast till brown specks appear on both sides.
- Spread a teaspoon of the green chutney on the roti and drizzle some chilli sauce and tomato sauce. Place one portion of the mince and some onion rings on the roti. Sprinkle lemon juice and chaat masala and roll up firmly.
- Serve immediately.

Chicken Wraps

Ingredients

2 (180 grams each) boneless chicken breasts

2 pita breads

2 tablespoons vinegar

1 tablespoon sugar

1 green chilli, chopped

1 small carrot, grated

1 small cabbage, shredded

1 small green capsicum, finely sliced

1 teaspoon ginger paste

1 teaspoon garlic paste

1 teaspoon cumin powder

1 teaspoon red chilli powder

1 tablespoon lemon juice

½ teaspoon soy sauce

1 egg, lightly beaten

¼ cup refined flour

¼ cup Mint Chutney (page 60)

1 medium onion, sliced into rings

Salt to taste

Oil for deep-frying

Method

- In a bowl, mix the vinegar, sugar, salt and green chilli thoroughly. Leave to stand for about half an hour or till the vinegar becomes a little spicy; strain the vinegar.
- Add the carrot, cabbage and green capsicum to the strained vinegar and toss well. Chill in a refrigerator till required.
- Cut the chicken into strips. In a bowl, mix the ginger paste, garlic paste, cumin powder, chilli powder, lemon juice, soy sauce, salt and egg. Add the chicken and flour and mix thoroughly. Set aside to marinate for half an hour, preferably in a refrigerator.
- Heat plenty of oil in a non-stick kadai. Deep-fry the chicken till cooked. Drain on absorbent paper.
- Heat both sides of the pita breads on a non-stick tawa or in an oven.
- Cut each pita bread in half and open out the pockets. Spread some mint chutney on the inside of each half, and fill with a portion each of chicken, vegetable mixture and onion rings. Serve immediately.

Mint Chutney

Grind 5 cups fresh mint, 3 cups fresh coriander, 10 green chillies, 3 onions, and 3 inches of ginger to a fine paste, adding a little water if required. Stir in 1 tablespoon lemon juice, salt and pomegranate seed powder.

Chicken Calzones

Ingredients

Pastry

2 cups refined flour
1 teaspoon fresh yeast
½ teaspoon sugar
Butter as required
½ teaspoon salt
1 tablespoon olive oil

Filling

2 chicken breasts, chopped
4 garlic cloves, chopped
2 medium onions, chopped
1 medium green capsicum, chopped
½ cup Tomato Concasse (page 96)
½ teaspoon red chilli flakes
½ teaspoon dried mixed herbs
1 jalapeño chilli, chopped
3-4 black peppercorns, crushed
Salt to taste
2 tablespoons olive oil

Method

- For the pastry, sift the refined flour with salt and make a well in the centre. Dissolve the yeast in lukewarm water along with some sugar and pour into the well. Mix.
- Make a soft dough using water as required. Cover with a damp piece of muslin and set aside at room temperature till it doubles in size.
- Preheat the oven to 200°C/400°F/Gas Mark 6. Grease a baking tray with one tablespoon olive oil.
- Knock back the dough lightly, divide into four equal portions and roll out each portion into a one-inch thick round. Set aside for about twenty minutes in a warm place.
- For the filling, heat the olive oil in a non-stick pan; add the garlic and sauté for one minute. Add the onions and continue to sauté till translucent.
- Add the capsicum and chicken and sauté for three to four minutes. Stir in the tomato concasse and cook till well blended. Add the chilli flakes, mixed herbs, jalapeño chilli, salt and crushed peppercorns. Mix well, remove from heat and set aside to cool.
- Divide the mixture into four portions and spread each portion over a pastry round. Fold over into a half-moon shape. Press the edges together to seal and place on the greased tray.
- Bake for about forty-five minutes till golden brown. Brush with melted butter and serve hot.

Fresh Rice Paper Rolls with Prawns

Ingredients

24 medium prawns, shelled and deveined

12 rice paper rounds each measuring 16 centimetres

1 teaspoon garlic paste

Black pepper powder to taste

1 cup finely shredded cabbage

½ cup coarsely grated carrot

2 tablespoons roughly chopped fresh mint

2 tablespoons roughly chopped fresh coriander

Salt to taste

2 tablespoons oil

Dipping sauce

⅓ cup caster sugar

¼ cup white vinegar

2 teaspoons fish sauce

2 fresh red chillies, sliced thinly

1 tablespoon finely chopped fresh coriander

Method

- Marinate the prawns in a mixture of garlic paste, salt and pepper powder for fifteen minutes.
- Heat the oil in a non-stick pan and toss the prawns till cooked. Set aside.
- Combine the cabbage, carrot, fresh mint and fresh coriander in a bowl.
- For the dipping sauce, heat sugar, vinegar and one-fourth cup of water in a small non-stick pan and stir until the sugar dissolves. Bring the mixture to a boil, remove from heat and add fish sauce and red chillies. Set aside to cool and add the fresh coriander.
- Soak the rice papers in water for one minute and place them on a serving plate.
- Divide the vegetable mixture equally into twelve portions and place in the centre of each round. Place two prawns over the vegetable mixture. Fold in the sides and roll to enclose the filling.
- Serve immediately with the dipping sauce.

Seekh Roti

Ingredients

For the filling

500 grams boneless mutton, cut into 1-inch cubes

4 tablespoons unripe green papaya paste

1 tablespoon garlic paste

½ tablespoon ginger paste

4-5 green chillies, chopped

1 tablespoon red chilli powder

½ tablespoon coriander powder

1 teaspoon roasted cumin powder

1 teaspoon garam masala powder

2 large onions, chopped

1 teaspoon poppy seeds

1 teaspoon sesame seeds

1½ tablespoons vinegar

Salt to taste

3 tablespoons ghee

To serve

8 roomali rotis

¼ cup Green Chutney (page 95)

2 large onions, sliced

2 tablespoons chopped fresh mint

Method

- In a large bowl, combine the mutton, papaya paste, garlic paste, ginger paste, green chillies, chilli powder, coriander powder, roasted cumin powder, garam masala powder and salt. Leave to marinate for four to five hours, preferably in a refrigerator.
- Heat two tablespoons ghee in a non-stick kadai; add the onion and sauté over medium heat till golden brown. Add the marinated mutton, stir and cook, uncovered, on low heat for ten minutes. Add half a cup of water, cover and cook for twenty to twenty-five minutes or till the mutton is tender. Add the poppy and sesame seeds and continue to cook, uncovered, for another fifteen minutes till all the water has evaporated. Stir in the vinegar, remove from heat and set aside.
- To obtain a smoky flavour, place a live piece of charcoal in a bowl and place the bowl in the centre of the mutton mixture. Pour one tablespoon of hot ghee on the charcoal, cover the pan immediately and leave to stand for three to four minutes. Remove the bowl with the charcoal from the mutton mixture.
- To prepare the wraps, divide the mutton mixture into eight equal portions. Place a roti on a plate and smear some green chutney over it. Spread a portion of the mutton mixture over the roti, sprinkle some sliced onions and fresh mint, roll up into a wrap and secure with a piece of aluminium foil.

Note: *Roomali roti can be replaced with large, thin whole-wheat roti.*

Hot Dogs

Ingredients

4 bread rolls
4 chicken sausages
2 tablespoons butter
4 tablespoons Mayonnaise (see below)
2 teaspoons mustard paste

Method

- Slit the bread rolls without cutting through. Heat the butter in a non-stick pan and sauté the chicken sausages for a minute. Drain and set aside.
- In the same pan, lightly warm the bread rolls. Place one sautéed sausage in each roll. Spread one tablespoon of mayonnaise and half a teaspoon of mustard paste.
- Serve immediately.

Mushroom and Leek Spring Rolls

Ingredients

10-15 button mushrooms, sliced
8-10 shiitake mushrooms, sliced
2 leeks, sliced
10 Spring Roll Wrappers (page 24)
1 cup glass noodles
6-8 garlic cloves, chopped
1 inch ginger, chopped
5-6 black peppercorns, crushed
7-8 spring onions with greens, chopped
1 egg, beaten
Sichuan Sauce (page 96)
Salt to taste
2 tablespoons oil + for deep-frying

Method

- Soak the glass noodles in three cups of hot water for two to three minutes. Drain thoroughly and spread on a plate to cool.
- Heat two tablespoons of oil in a non-stick wok and sauté the garlic and ginger.

- Add all the mushrooms, leeks, salt, crushed peppercorns and sauté until the moisture dries up. Remove from heat and set aside to cool. Stir in the spring onions and glass noodles.
- To assemble the rolls, place two tablespoons of the mixture in the centre of each spring roll wrapper and fold one side over the filling. Fold both the parallel sides over leaving the fourth side open. Brush the edge with some beaten egg and roll up tightly.
- Heat sufficient oil in a wok and deep-fry the spring rolls till golden brown. Drain on absorbent paper.
- Serve hot with Sichuan sauce.

Sausage Triangles

Ingredients

200 grams chicken sausages, chopped

2 medium potatoes, boiled, peeled and mashed

4 sheets filo pastry

1 large onion, grated

2 garlic cloves, chopped

5-6 black peppercorns, crushed
1 egg, beaten lightly
Salt to taste
3 teaspoons oil

Method

- Preheat the oven to 220°C/425°F/Gas Mark 7.
- Heat the oil in a small non-stick pan; add the onion and garlic and sauté till translucent. Transfer to a bowl.
- Add the mashed potatoes and sausages and mix well. Add salt and the crushed peppercorns and mix again.
- Cut each pastry sheet in half. Divide the sausage mixture equally among the pastry halves, placing it at one end of the pastry sheet. Brush the beaten egg mixture around the edges and fold into triangles.
- Place the triangles on a lightly oiled baking tray. Bake, uncovered, for about twenty-five minutes, or until lightly browned. Serve hot.

Chilli-Chicken Croissants

Ingredients

Croissant

4 cups refined flour + for dusting

2½ tablespoons milk powder

2 teaspoons salt

1 tablespoon fresh yeast

3 tablespoons sugar

1¼ cups butter

1 egg, beaten

Filling

200 grams chicken fillets, roughly chopped

150 grams chicken salami, roughly chopped

1 garlic clove, finely chopped

1 small onion, chopped

1 teaspoon paprika

½ teaspoon oregano

2 tablespoons finely chopped fresh coriander

2 stalks spring onion greens, finely chopped

Salt to taste

1 tablespoon oil

Method

- In a bowl, mix together four cups of flour, milk powder and salt. Dissolve yeast and sugar in half cup of warm water and allow it to stand for fifteen minutes. Keep butter in deep freezer for chilling.
- Add the yeast mixture to the flour. Add three-fourth cup water and knead into a smooth dough. Keep the dough, covered with a damp muslin, in a warm place to rise for thirty to forty minutes.
- Slice the chilled butter into thin slices.
- Knock back the dough and roll into a forty centimetre by seventy centimetre rectangle using a little flour for dusting. Brush off the excess flour.
- Arrange the chilled butter on two-thirds of the rectangle in the centre. Fold the uncovered one-third part over to the centre and bring over the remaining one-third part to make a book fold. Seal the sides well so that the butter does not come out.
- Roll the pastry again to the same size and make a book fold. Keep in the refrigerator for half an hour covered in cling film so that no moisture goes in.
- Repeat the process twice without the butter. Again roll the dough into a rectangle of the same size and trim the sides.

- For the filling, heat oil in a non-stick pan and sauté the garlic and onion till translucent. Add the chicken fillets and salami and stir-fry till chicken is cooked but still juicy. Add salt, paprika, oregano, fresh coriander and spring onion greens and toss. Set aside.
- Cut the rectangular dough into two strips, lengthwise, with a sharp knife. Further cut into large triangles with each side measuring approximately fifteen centimetres.
- Place the triangles on a lightly floured surface. Place one tablespoon of chicken mixture at the base of the triangle. Roll it in the shape of a crescent.
- Arrange on a baking tray, lightly brush with the beaten egg and leave to rise in a warm, humid place for thirty minutes or till doubled in size.
- Preheat the oven to 200°C/400°F/Gas Mark 6.
- Bake the croissants in the preheated oven for fifteen minutes. Reduce the temperature to 190°C/375°F/Gas Mark 5 and further bake for ten minutes. Serve hot.

Chicken Rolls

Ingredients

2 (250 grams) chicken breasts, boiled and shredded

4 hot dog rolls

½ cup Mayonnaise (page 95)

1 garlic clove, chopped

1 tablespoon tomato ketchup

1 tablespoon mustard paste

Black pepper powder to taste

A few lettuce leaves, to garnish

Salt to taste

Method

- Place the mayonnaise, garlic, tomato ketchup, mustard paste, salt, pepper powder and shredded chicken in a bowl and mix well. Divide into four portions.
- Slit the hot dog rolls but do not cut through.
- Line the rolls with lettuce leaves and spread one portion of the chicken mixture on the bottom half of each roll and press the top half down lightly. Secure with a toothpick and serve immediately.

Moussaka Crêpes

Ingredients

Crêpes

½ cup refined flour
1 egg
1 tablespoon butter + for greasing
1 cup milk
½ cup Cheese Sauce (page 95)

Filling

1 small brinjal, diced
250 grams minced mutton
4 tablespoons butter
6 shallots
½ teaspoon dried oregano
1 garlic clove, crushed
2 tomatoes, blanched, peeled and chopped
2 teaspoons tomato paste
Black pepper powder to taste
½ cup fresh breadcrumbs
2 tablespoons grated Parmesan cheese
½ cup Cheese Sauce (page 95)
Salt to taste
2 tablespoons oil

Method

- For the crêpes, sift the refined flour into a bowl. Add the egg, one tablespoon melted butter and two tablespoons of milk. Beat until smooth.
- Add the remaining milk a little by little to make a smooth batter. Set aside for thirty minutes.
- Heat a non-stick frying pan over medium heat; lightly grease it with butter and pour two to three tablespoons of batter into the pan. Rotate the pan so that the batter spreads all around.
- Cook over low heat until the batter has set and lightly browned underneath. Turn and brown the other side as well.
- Remove the crêpe and set aside on a plate. Repeat with the remaining batter. Keep the crêpes warm.
- Preheat the oven to 180°C/350°F/Gas Mark 4.
- For the filling, sprinkle the brinjal pieces with one teaspoon salt and set aside for thirty minutes. Rinse under cold water and drain on absorbent paper.
- Heat the oil in non-stick pan; add the minced mutton and sauté for ten minutes. Remove from the pan and set aside.

- Melt the butter in the same pan. Add the brinjal, shallots, oregano and garlic and cook for one minute. Add the tomatoes, tomato paste and pepper powder and cook for one minute.
- Transfer to a bowl and add the sautéed lamb, the breadcrumbs, Parmesan cheese and half a cup of cheese sauce. Mix thoroughly and adjust the seasoning.
- Place two tablespoons of filling at one end of each crêpe and roll up, tucking in the sides.
- Arrange the crêpes in a shallow eleven-inch square ovenproof dish. Pour the cheese sauce over and bake, uncovered, for fifteen minutes.
- Remove from the oven and serve warm.

Shawarma

Ingredients

4 (180 grams each) chicken breasts
4 pita breads
Salt to taste
4 tablespoons olive oil

Yogurt sauce

1 cup yogurt
1 teaspoon garlic paste
2 tablespoons lemon juice
1 sprig fresh parsley
Salt to taste

Salad

1 medium onion, sliced
1 medium tomato, sliced
2 jalapeño chillies, sliced
2 tablespoons tahini
3 tablespoons yogurt
6-8 fresh mint, roughly torn
Salt to taste

Method

- For the yogurt sauce, add the salt and garlic paste to the yogurt and whisk well. Stir in the lemon juice. Spoon the mixture into a piece of muslin placed over a bowl, gather the edges and squeeze tightly to get a thick, smooth yogurt sauce. Garnish with a sprig of parsley and set aside.
- Preheat the oven to 200°C/400°F/Gas Mark 6.
- Slit the chicken breasts lengthways without cutting through. Drizzle olive oil over them, sprinkle salt and thread them in folds onto a skewer. Place the skewer on a rotisserie (rotating rack). Place the rotisserie in the preheated oven and cook for twenty minutes.
- Remove from the oven and slice the chicken into thin pieces while still on the skewer.
- Toast the pita breads lightly on a non-stick tawa or in an oven. Slit them open to form pockets.
- For the 'salad', mix together the onion, tomato, jalapeños, salt, tahini, yogurt and fresh mint. Stuff the pita pocket with some of the sliced chicken mixture and top with the onion-tomato salad.
- Serve immediately with the yogurt sauce.

Mawa Rolls

Ingredients

Pancakes

1 cup refined flour

A pinch of salt

½ teaspoon baking powder

½ teaspoon soda bicarbonate

1½ tablespoons powdered sugar

¼ cup grated, khoya/mawa

1 cup milk

Ghee for greasing

Filling

800 grams khoya/mawa, grated

¼ cup milk

10 tablespoons powdered sugar

1½ teaspoons green cardamom powder

50 pistachios, roughly chopped

50 almonds, roughly chopped

Method

- For the pancakes, sieve refined flour, salt, baking powder, soda bicarbonate and sugar in a bowl. Add the grated khoya and mix. Add milk and mix well. Ensure that there are no lumps. Adjust the consistency by adding more milk. Heat the ghee in a non-stick pan. Pour a ladleful of the batter and spread to a medium thickness.

- Cook till done on one side then flip and cook on the other side. Transfer onto a plate and set aside.
- For the filling, heat a non-stick kadai, add grated khoya, milk and powdered sugar and cook till soft. Add cardamom powder, pistachios and almonds and mix. Take the mixture off the heat.
- Place a pancake on a plate. Spread a little of the filling and roll. Make more rolls with the remaining batter and filling. Cut the rolls diagonally in the middle and serve hot.

Pancakes Filled with Sweet Coconut

Ingredients

1¼ cups desiccated coconut

½ cup brown sugar

1 pandan leaf, stripped through with a fork and tied into a knot

A pinch of salt

Pancake batter

1 cup refined flour

A pinch of salt

1 egg, beaten

A few drops of vanilla essence

4 teaspoons oil + for frying

Method

- Pour one cup of water into a non-stick pan. Add the sugar and stir to dissolve. Add the pandan leaf and cook over low heat, stirring continuously. Bring the mixture to a boil, and continue to cook for three to four minutes, or till syrupy but not caramelised.
- Put the coconut in a non-stick wok along with a pinch of salt. Pour the sugar mixture over, and cook over low heat, stirring occasionally, for five to seven minutes, or till the mixture becomes almost dry. Set aside.
- To make the pancake batter, blend together the flour, a pinch of salt, egg, vanilla essence and one cup of water and whisk till smooth. Add oil and whisk till the oil is incorporated.
- Lightly grease a non-stick frying pan; pour a ladleful of the batter and swirl to spread the batter evenly. Cook till done.
- Place a generous helping of the filling in the centre of each pancake, roll up and serve immediately.

Swiss Rolls

Ingredients

¾ cup refined flour
½ teaspoon baking powder
4 eggs, separated
¾ cup powdered sugar, sifted
1 teaspoon vanilla essence
¼ teaspoon salt
2 teaspoons caster sugar, for dusting
5 tablespoons mixed fruit jam

Method

- Preheat the oven to 190°C/375°F/Gas Mark 5. Line a fifteen-inch by ten-inch baking tray with greased thick, unglazed brown paper.
- Sift the flour with baking powder. Beat the egg yolks until light. Continue beating the mixture, adding the sugar gradually, till creamy. Stir in the vanilla essence.
- Gently and gradually fold in the flour into the egg mixture. Beat the batter until smooth.
- Whip the egg whites with salt until stiff, but not dry. Fold in the egg whites lightly into the batter.

- Spread the batter in the prepared tray and bake for about twelve minutes.
- While still hot, turn the cake out onto a sheet of greaseproof paper, sprinkled with caster sugar. Trim the hard edges. Spread the jam on the cake and carefully roll it up. Wrap the roll in the greaseproof paper.
- Allow to rest for half-an-hour. Remove the paper gently. Cut the cake into slices and serve.

Cinnamon Rolls

Ingredients

Dough

4 cups refined flour

2¼ teaspoons yeast

⅓ cup sugar

2 eggs

⅓ cup butter, melted

½ cup sour cream

1 teaspoon vanilla essence

Salt to taste

Oil to grease

Filling

2 teaspoons cinnamon powder
1 cup brown sugar
1 teaspoon nutmeg powder
3 tablespoons soft butter + for greasing
½ cup raisins
½ cup walnuts, chopped

Method

- Place yeast and one teaspoon of sugar in a mixing bowl. Add a quarter cup warm water and stir. Let the mixture stand for five to ten minutes or until it is frothy.
- Add the remaining sugar, eggs, butter, sour cream, vanilla essence and salt. Mix well. Add two cups of flour and mix well. Stir in the remaining flour, one fourth cup at a time, until the dough sticks together but is not dry.
- Place the dough on a lightly floured surface. Knead for about five minutes, or until the dough is smooth. Grease a bowl, place the dough in it, coat it with a little oil, cover with a cling film or damp towel and place in a warm place for about one and a half hours or till it doubles in volume.
- Beat back the dough with your fists. Place it back on the floured surface and knead for one minute. Cover the dough with a towel and let it rest till the filling is ready.

- For the filling, mix together the cinnamon, brown sugar and nutmeg powder in a small bowl.
- Lightly dust the rolling pin with flour and roll the dough into a rectangle about thirty by sixty centimetres. Spread three tablespoons butter all over the dough. Sprinkle the sugar mixture, raisins and nuts. Press the nuts and raisins lightly into the dough with the back of a wooden spoon.
- Starting at the narrow end, roll the dough as tightly as you can towards the other end. Pinch the seam to seal it. Cut the roll diagonally into twelve equal pieces.
- Grease a baking tray well with butter. Arrange the pieces, cut side down, in the tray. Cover tightly with a plastic wrap. Place in a warm place for about one and a half hours or till the pieces double in size.
- Preheat oven to 150°C/300°F/Gas Mark 2. Bake the rolls in the preheated oven for thirty minutes or until golden brown.
- Serve hot or at room temperature.

Oat Pancakes with Dried Fruit

Ingredients

⅛ cup oatmeal

¼ cup refined flour

¼ cup whole-wheat flour

A pinch of soda bicarbonate

A pinch of baking powder

1 tablespoon powdered sugar

1½ eggs

½ cup buttermilk

⅛ cup milk

A few drops of vanilla essence

1 tablespoon oil + for shallow-frying

Filling

2 tablespoons butter

½ cup dates, chopped

15 cashew nuts, chopped

15 pistachios, chopped

15 almonds, chopped

¾ cup maple syrup

Method

- Sift together both types of flour, soda bicarbonate and baking powder into a bowl.
- Add the powdered sugar and mix. Add the eggs and mix again. Add the buttermilk and mix well to make a smooth batter.
- Add oatmeal and milk and mix. Add a little oil and vanilla essence and mix well.
- To make the filling, melt butter in a non-stick pan and toss all the dried fruit in it for two to three minutes. Transfer into a bowl and let it cool a bit. Add maple syrup and mix.
- Heat a non-stick pan, grease it with a little oil. Pour a ladleful of batter and spread evenly on the pan. Drizzle a little oil all round and let it cook on medium heat for two minutes. Flip and cook on the other side.
- Place a little of the filling on one side of the pancake and roll it up.
- Serve hot.

Basic recipes

Cheese Sauce

Melt 2 tablespoons of butter in a pan; add 2 tablespoons of refined flour and cook over low heat for a few minutes. Gradually stir in 2 cups of warm milk, and stir continuously till thick. Stir in 1 cup of grated cheese, white pepper powder and salt to taste. Cook till the cheese melts.

Green Chutney

Grind together 1 cup fresh coriander, ½ cup fresh mint, 2-3 green chillies, black salt to taste, ¼ teaspoon sugar and 1 tablespoon lemon juice to a smooth paste using a little water if required.

Mayonnaise

Place 1 egg yolk, salt to taste, ¼ teaspoon each white pepper powder, mustard powder and sugar and 1 teaspoon vinegar in a clean bowl and mix thoroughly with a whisk. Alternatively, process the mixture in a blender. Add 1 cup of oil, a little at a time, whisking or blending continuously, until all the oil is incorporated. Add 1 teaspoon lemon juice and adjust seasoning. Store in an airtight jar in a refrigerator.

Sichuan Sauce

Boil 10-12 dried red chillies in one cup of water for five to seven minutes. Drain, cool and grind to a fine paste. Heat ½ cup oil in a pan and add 10 garlic cloves, peeled and finely chopped, 2 finely chopped green chillies, 2 finely chopped spring onions and 1-inch peeled and grated ginger. Sauté for a minute, then add the red chilli paste and sauté a bit more. Add a 2-3 inch celery stalk, 3 tablespoons tomato ketchup and salt to taste. Stir well to mix. Stir in 2 teaspoons white vinegar and simmer for a minute. Take the pan off the heat when the oil rises to the surface. Cool and store. Sichuan sauce will keep for a month if there is sufficient oil covering the surface.

Tomato Concasse

Blanch and peel four medium tomatoes, remove seeds and chop finely.

Makes one cup.

Vegetable Stock

Peel, wash and chop 1 onion, ½ medium carrot, 3-inch celery stalk and 2-3 garlic cloves. Place in a non-stick pan with 1 bay leaf, 5-6 peppercorns, 2-3 cloves and five cups of water and bring to a boil. Lower heat and simmer for fifteen minutes and strain. Cool and store in a refrigerator till further use.